CW00966788

PRESSURE PRESS PRESENTS
The FACEBOOK Group Collection

GOSS183 Publishing Group
Copyright © 2014 Pressure Press Contributors
Bloomington, Illinois

When the idea to create and publish this collection arose, I hesitated. I knew the amount of work and time it took to complete the massive project, and I balked. I found myself trying to talk myself out of doing such a thing, based on experience; most poets are plain insane when it comes to publishing their work. But I was in good company, since the requisite for submission was membership in *Pressure Press Presents,* my members-only Facebook group.

Community is the solid platform on which we build. I consider all the contributors here my friends, some pure family. *Pressure Press Presents* rocks and boils and keeps me cranked – cranked as an editor, too. In the spirit of the group's name, I am glad to open more awareness of those presented here, a collection of writers who span the visions of modern poetry like a lake horizon.

Thanks to Ann Androla, Didi Menendez, Chuck Joy, and all of the wonderful people who sent in work for consideration.

Thanks for the Internet.

Thanks for language surprises.

Thanks for soul communication and epiphanies.

Ron Androla, Editor
October 2014

PRESSURE PRESS

EDITED BY
**Ron
Androla**

Front Cover by
Jeff Filipski

contributors

Adrian C. Louis

Varykino: Status update

My feet are cracked & bleeding. Ice spiders got to them last night. Now they are swollen & I can't get my boots on. I wrap them in old t-shirts & trudge through the snow to the computer shack. The shack is frozen from stem to stern. I smash a chair, set it afire, & thaw out the brittle computer. No x-rated email from Yuriatin. Another boiled potato day with Tonya...

Adrian C. Louis

Poison Ivy

Town's too tawdry for a sunny day so
I drive to Garvin State Park & tramp
around the woods near a stream, note
tall birches with poison ivy trailing up
into the branches, the leaves bright red
in early autumn & then I cruise back
to town, go to the tattoo parlor &
have them ink my entire body with
red ivy leaves, even my dinger &
then a week or two later I go back to
the park & stand naked in front
of the climbing ivy & wait for folks
to amble by—I plan to grab them &
shout, "Ivy loves you," but I look
at the ivy & it is no longer red,
the leaves have yellowed, fallen
to the ground, so I fall down too,
my yellow heart gently itching
& rattling towards winter.

Adrian C. Louis

To an Indian Cowboy in the Nursing Home

To hell with these high school
dropouts who call themselves aides.
They ain't aiding anything at all.
Cousin, don't let the bastards
slather Hollandaise upon
the feral flesh of our earth.
Don't let them mutter
colonial anthems in your
dark cavern of senility.
Stand straight, remember,
yes, remember how
we rode those bulls
in bright sunshine
& screwed them
ever so gently
as the margarine
of moonlight reflected
off our tinfoil war bonnets.

The Plastic Poem

so far
plastic is our
greatest creation

i mean
fuck stone -
plastic's gonna last
even longer

in the middle
of every ocean
on earth
right now

that swirling place
out center
where all our sea currents
go to die

there are these islands
massive islands
islands of plastic garbage
grooving themselves together

& forming into monstrous rocks
that even salt water
cannot sink

Patrick Mckinnon

poem for steven's fingers

whenever steven's
hands are freezin'
his hands go down his pants
'cuz its warmer there than armpits
or pockets
or underneath his sitting ass
it's 8 below zero
before even christmas
& steven's a dulutheran
who understands the
ice waterfall city, minnesota cold
tells people often
that "in 1978
there were 80,000 folks up here
& in 2014
the number is still the same"
calls it "population control"
as he grabs his own nuts...
the only beachy spot
on his frosted november body
palms are fine

its always just the fingers
those ice-blood little sticks
sez he'd cut the stiff things off
if he didn't "need 'em
so goddamn much"
warming steven's head &
heating steven's feet are necessary
but as easy as that drunk chick
he met @ quinlan's club on sunday nite
compared to reinvigorating
his hands
"it all started
w/a bowl of hawaiian
& a back rub" sez
"my fingers that night
thawed out
one freezing female spine"

PRESSURE PRESS COLLECTION 2014

Cheryl Townsend

As It Is

I have reached the age

where a giggle has the tendency

to be moist and the hairs

that now sprout in the most

unflattering of places must be

plucked by grandchildren who

can still see that close

I don't unfold like I used to

but still manage to tie my own shoes

without need of chair or elevated assistance

The volume has increased on the TV and

there is much repetition in conversations

When I unhook the back of my bra

it no longer falls to the floor

but stays put - tucked tight under

pendulous breasts with nipples

that point the way for the rest

of my body to follow

But I am here
Long free of parental animosity
Past the angry marriage of youth
Beyond the cancer of promiscuity
Away from the semi lights that should've
but just barely didn't
And the debauchery of fluid ignorance

I am here
And I speak with contemplation
Listen with intention and give
like there's no tomorrow
After all, I may indeed be here
but who can guarantee I'll also
be there

She Finds Herself Dancing

In another universe, a hand touches a great machine. There is a button which, when pressed, brings motion and light. With that, the world begins. Again.

* * * * * * * * * * *

The visions come when Mary dances. When she's talking to her grandpa or the servants, or hatching a plan with her plucky friend, Louise, to keep from being taken to an orphan's home, she's too caught up in the problems of the world. But when she dances! That's when she feels free and alive and the visions come and, of a sudden, she holds the dim, impossible memory that this has happened many times before. The visions are always the same, only with changing faces.

Always, she sees a dark room, large, and filled with people. They sit in row after ordered row and it's a little creepy, the way they stare at her, but she likes it, too. It feels like this is what she's made for. She finds it odd that some of them eat handfuls of something they pull from boxes on their laps, and occasionally she gets embarrassed because she notices a couple, usually toward the back of the room, kissing and touching one another in a way that would surely give Grandpa fits. But none of this makes her stop dancing. In fact, she never misses a step.

Which is funny, because the dances are impromptu and complicated and sometimes done with an unexpected partner: Jubilee, the butler; plucky Louise; her old grandpa; even Napoleon, the Great Dane that Grandpa loves to curse, but secretly feeds scraps from the table when he doesn't think anyone is around. She's considering this as Jubilee demonstrates a mean soft shoe and then points to her, clearly meaning that now it's her turn to do the same moves, or maybe something better, and how in the blue fucking hell could he expect her to do this, as she's never done the first soft shoe in her life? But, lacking a choice, she surrenders to her body and her steps are flawless. It makes no sense.

And then, there it is, the crowd. She allows herself to consider the word, "audience." There must be two hundred people out there, watching her. She's glad to know she can't possibly fail, but that certainty removes some of the luster from the thrill of the performance.

About twenty-five rows back, a boy and a girl sit close together. His arm drapes her shoulders and she molds to his body like still water along a smooth lake bank. They aren't like other couples she's seen, so desperate and obvious. She sees them like this and feels a vacancy in her heart.

The boy and girl hold her attention for a while, but inevitably she notices the light. How did she miss it until now? The light is brilliant and, now that she has realized it is there, all-encompassing. It is more important than all the faces, more important than the couple she was watching. She realizes she is of the light, sustained by it, but still a separate entity, just as Jubilee is separate and Grandpa and Louise.

Everything. But if everything is of the light, then everything must ultimately be the same. Not made of the same thing, or really, really similar, but the same one thing. Damn, that's confusing, but it seems to be the only honest answer. Mary wants to know the oneness of returning to the source.

Maybe this light tells her story again and again. Why wouldn't it? Maybe it brings forth other worlds, just as real as hers, but impossible to visit. If it can illuminate one world, why not an infinite number of worlds that loop through time? Beginning, living, ending, beginning again. And what if there are other lights? This is all too much. Mary's stomach starts to churn. Maybe this is what freedom feels like.

With every step, every smile, she tries to pull herself out of the moment which now she understands to be endlessly repeating. She tries to pull outside of herself and return. Return. She feels dizzy, blissful, and terrified, remorseful at her separation from the source. And then she feels the beginning of separation from the place in which she seems to exist and the tug toward merging with the light. But it is never enough. Once, she believes, she almost made it, found herself for the smallest moment in a blazing, white-hot universe and wondered if this were heaven or hell.

Does Jubilee have these visions? Louise? Napoleon? Anyone? When Jubilee picks her up and throws her toward the ceiling, she spinning in mid-air, he catching her as she falls, is he trying to push her through to this new world? Does he know it is impossible? Is that why his eyes look so sad and full of love above that brilliant smile?

Just as an answer begins forming in her mind, she stomps her left foot onto the floor a good ten inches in front of her right and extends both arms forty-five degrees from her body, palms forward and fingers splayed. The dance is over.

Almost as soon as she is still, the vision is gone. Like each of the countless times before, once the vision leaves, she forgets she has had it. What remains is the vacancy in her heart that she cannot now fathom. If only she could tell someone, Louise maybe, but whom she talks to, what she says, these things follow a path of their own design. After a while she puts away the ache, hides it until it really seems to be gone. And then, for no good reason, she finds herself dancing.

The Bottoms

his brother shot Gina Brook in the face
with a brick bone automatic in his apartment
above Sally's hair salon
she was sleeping with Timmy Teeth
discreetly but word got out
and Bobby with his voices took his demon tanks
down a mud path in his brain
he grabbed a load of cobble stone
and paved a wall in the attic
sealing her body in the crawl space.
when the police knocked it down
flies were crawling out of her nostrils.
Timmy Teeth was found in the river
rocks in his pockets
half his head like a Zippo lighter
flapping in the current
his eyeball like an under cooked egg
on his chin

they say the sickness is in the family
his father was all blood and brandy
and the mother used to drown rats in the spring
but ole little Joey never hurt no one

you can see him on the train bridge
singing Jesus Jews and infidels
he buys cigars and sweet tea
swallows pills and mint leaves
blames the doctors
for hammering his mind out
into the sun

John Korn

Yellow Lamp Shade Day

On the corner of Granson Street

old people sit hunched inside

group home with thin memories,

wall papered walls

wheel chair drugged solidarity.

Dust particles swim around eyes

television voices seem deranged here.

Obscene screams from "The Price Is Right"

don't register on 80 year old faces.

I leave Mr. Grotto next to the window.

His back is too bad. Can't live on his own anymore.

I don't want to leave him there. It's the end of the line.

They will drug him into a puddle of half sleep.

He will lay in bed and watch the curtains breathe in and out.

When I pull the van away

he falls out of my head. And I drive home.

Nap on my couch. Lamp shade head.

Voices of the neighbors below seep into my dreams.

Could be old memories. I could be in a nursing home

reliving all this in a drugged daze.

PRESSURE PRESS COLLECTION 2014

Scabby Babby

Scabby Babby they used to call her.

She had that skin condition.

Had these little scabs all over her neck and face.

Always pickin' at em.

Like an ape that woman.

Sad. Dragged her feet.

She used to collect hub caps and old car parts

off the road and make these weird

wind chimes by tying them to the branches

of the trees in her yard.

Sometimes if you drove by her house at night

you could see her silhouetted bulk in the window upstairs.

Looking slumped and heavy.

She dragged Dennis Doobey

out of Henry's bar

one night into the parking lot.

Kicked him around.

He looked like a straw dummy.

Then she stepped on the back of his head.

Grinded his face in the gravel.

He fucked her I guess then was ignoring her cause he was too embarrassed

to let anyone know.

18

So she let everyone know.

Shit. Man, that was long ago.
I see all these faces now.
You know when you're looking down
at a pot of stew and it just looks like broth?
But then you stir it then up out of the murkiness comes
bits of meat and carrot and potatoes?
That's what my mind is like now.
My chest feels like an old box
with a dead mouse inside.
I wake up early
like 5 or 4 am.
I sit there in my bed just smoking
watching the sun come up.
It's a strange shade of blue that early.
It was like that when we sunk
Babby into the lake that morning.
Her face all frozen.
Eyes bugging out.
Dennis tied a few cinder blocks to her feet.
I remember when she sunk
there was that sound of water
pouring into her mouth.

Pawn Shopped Prepositions at 3:16 A.M

Arbitrary rumors of people from your past
on the bus, eavesdropped.

How they follow you, you run your hand
through your hair arcade childhood addicts

basement twitching scratching my arms
the rough otherness of figures.

What is memory but within the distance
touching you? All the frequencies of go on

drop dead. The Drop Kick Murphy's
punching out the wall of that apartment.

The eclipse of your own face.
The burden is a kind of rope

with a bucket of lead, pulling
you down into a well,

where you waited for no one to come.
Perhaps it is better to speak

to these silhouettes, the shadow puppets
of your hands? You move them over a crack

in the wall, asking them to show you the map
to what you have lost. Blue petals

blown from somewhere on the sill.
Tell it in contrails. The endlessly running faucet.

Someone straggling across the street,
you can see them, the matchstick

figure outlined against the flaming haze.
High in daylight like thieves.

This searching through morphine's
black orchids. It is so hard to describe,

like a detective reading the clues
to a crime (wanting clarity),

to cross a suspension bridge
along the coast and find this foghorn

incantation, this rococo reckoning,
this red velvet box of oneself

both jewel case and coffin.

Sean Thomas Dougherty

Opening Shift at the Pool Hall

Off to vacuum the ash
burned pool hall carpet,

wipe down the green
felt tables, wipe away

the scratches and the miscues.
Wipe drunken finger smudges

from the windows and pull down
the shades to keep the sunlight out.

Dump the swill bucket.
Mop the floor of boot scuffs

and spilled drinks. Take away
all the human mistakes: *it is what I do.*

So the Seraphim may descend.
So when someone lifts a cue

on a sleepy Saturday afternoon,
anything can happen—

with the simple stroke of an arm
and an eye that sees beyond

the present: Blue chalk to tip, aim,
and then the hard clack— a line
emerges, an axis, traveling
like a comet across the cosmos

of clean felt. Till after spinning
three rails, the ball falls

into the pocket's dark—
And in the far corner, Gabriel,

that old rail-bird, rustling
his feathers, and quietly chuckling—

Massachusetts

Tonight I feel you Ellen
through thirty years of distance

red wine, weed & Percocet
birds in kitchen cages

Irish shoulder to the wheel
but things break anyway

I keep thinking Massachusetts
something faded, something with a girl.

Dad These Days

Curled like a question mark
a life outlives itself

we watch Jeopardy
I feed him what they bring

blue-eyed bone confusion
rattling the halls

I walk away, he calls for God
the elevator smells like piss.

Keep It Close

Cricket wishes on a star
then a bumpy streetcar home

six years old, me & mom
at the movies

cricket in the hearth
blessings on this house

keep it close son
dream me when I'm gone.

Dave Roskos

It's Mardi Gras time in my Frontal Lobe

i laid down in the grass on my back
& looked up at the sky
a little bug walked up
& sed "open up yr ear door
& let me in your head
& i'll spin a yarn
& turn a tale
like a tv tube rainbow flood
of visions caught in a
rain soaked spider web
between two trees
in a botanical garden
near the land of the dead.
    the flying turtles
            from damnation alley
                they be selling
 their lily pad souls
      to the vulture devils
            for a piece of salmon"

So i sed "okay bug, i'll open my
ear door, if ya promise
not to start no fires
in my frontal lobe"

"You call this poetry?"

I raised my eyebrows

"It doesn't even rhyme
and the stories, these people
they aren't nice
they have no redeeming
value to teach
they don't change
they're miserable."

I open my notebook
and begin to write.

"What are you doing?"

"I'm writing a poem
about you."

John Burroughs

Smoker

your nose

Streisand

your hair

Minnelli

your legs bare

your left

knee skinned

your pussy

ashtray hot

perhaps full

of stubs but

I don't care

because it's

Broadway and I

crave your lips

until you pull out

another cigarette

Festival of the Frozen Guy

Every spring, the beaten villages of the snow belt come out and search the thawing banks of concretion, ice and salt, rocks, bottles, tires, and the revealed body, starkly white or uncommon blue, his eyes open to the sky, perhaps. Perhaps he wears ratty plaid, or nothing at all, bare skin beginning to dry and change from the way it had remained since the snow came. Never does he tell how he got there, whether helped by an officious fender, or wind, a belly either too empty or too full, veins thickened or thinned. Helped to his feet first like a mannequin, then carried through shade to preserve him, we bring the carcass to the celebration grounds. Fires are made, none let come too close by the passing lord of winter. A-dancing, in hope of the coming season, the energetic ones cut the flesh in long shallow wounds, sewn with hope and respect, while the fecundity of rot, long slowed, unstoppered, begins to ripen. The young ones twirl the soft digits until the old ones hush them, rush them away before they make of the swelling thing a piñata. With hushed breath they listen at the corpse for songs and secrets of what's to come.

30

Jeremiah Walton

Eyedeas:

Shadow of the man you wish you are

Someone told me I'm brave
I told them I'm just bored

Listening like a knife to those midnight murmurs
meant for no ears

bruises cover the light in you

Even if it breaks me
I'll sacrifice my life for life

There's pain under every rug
under the core of every perspective

When I don't project the bullshit from within
& move through time's natural process
There's a glimmer
in the river
of a light I want to harbor in my shimmer

of existence.

Let childhood remain dead with its noose composed
of dreams

It's gone. Stop trying so hard
to hold on.

The corpse dangles in breeze
written on memories I won't let go of

Fuck off, let me grow up

Hitting the ground I walk under the shadow of the
man dangling that I wish I was

6th & Nicollet

it was the late 70's
he stood on a box
on the corner of 6th & nicollet
a tall older black man
calling out the name of the Lord

never heard more than a couple
words
all i needed to hear
to know he was preaching

he had a big round bump
on his forehead
every year it got bigger

he was there in the morning
when i went to work
he was there when i went
out for lunch
and he was still there
when i went home at night

calling out urgently
at the top of his lungs

one day
i can't tell you when
i didn't see him anymore
i'm not sure if he moved
to another block
or if he walked into the light

White Noise Dream

It sounds like record
player needle dropped
to vinyl,

pop and hiss.

In the jaguar of this,
mauve and jade green voices
thread across computer monitor.

They sound like creep strangers,
huffing and blowing over phone lines

until the words:

im sorry im sorry
for my mistakes -

audible, heartbeat apology.

The dream leads
to beach where

waves rolling in

sound like tv static.

Where someone down sand calls out
(voice like thin blue line):

Where are you going?

When will you return?

Marisa Moks-Unger

Union Dues

Within war production years
immigrant maidens wound coils
for bombers, tanks, ammunition.

From Antonia's wages flowed
a cold-water flat, groats, kishka, plums
for ailing parents, a bevy of kin -
not a wedding gown.

The sepia photo of that day
shows her regal in glowing silk,
her spouse in tie and tails

all rented for an hour to
weld golden orbs and vows in
second-hand studio splendor.

Gifts and Their Trajectories

you look so very tired
provocateur, gun for hire
I'll do it for you
wade into the the oil slick surf
past the regret of dying birds
out to the curling water
return your dirge in a bottle
though you meant it for god's mother
her pathogens and blood borne
children, her expansive hunger
to whet the grief
of apathetic rerun watchers
old and sick and thin
with no appetite for life

I've no lust or luck left
only parts settled by dust
calcium deposits
thin blue blood
wicked and burning lower
lower
rags on rags
this dress of bleached flowers
it is not my house
not my funeral bower
the sea, she gave you up
it is enough, this longing for
even a single note
evidence of song
the singer
stilled

Lunch with Frank O'Hara

There was a magnificence that protruded between
time and light.
We thought radical was in a healing mode.
Watered down beyond chaos
and scoping toward nonchalance.

We forgot the truth.
Assumed that virtue would take hold
at some point
and relegate us to rationality.

You didn't have to look too closely
to find the subjectivity
that blinded the rememberers
who could no longer quote the date.

Sycophants and starving elephants.
A ride to the park
past the Bronx Zoo.
Things we never saw at the time.

There was a hamburger stand
whose emblem was a coach-whip snake.
Standard fare was mustard and chili.
That was enough.

Intercept

My cloud lines burgeon these quaffed afternoons.
I hear a xylophone, a coin rolled down the keys.
The dress-made color in your eyes, and oak wind,
supple to the texture of refinement of a style. I glyph
alongside headway, claim we are approaching
an eviction of a presence in some garb the color
garden. Silk on flowers in a row sifts light intended
to stem growth. Many verses sung replay the light
of lime. The resurrection of this body loans idea to
mere surface. A song with whispered male voice
backgrounded by emotive blend dissuades the love
of a leftover self, having disowned its innocence.

Showcase, lower decibels, the infant skin unchanged

Potential

Which flat
of blooms
once over
turned a choir
"held harmless"
under fractal
moon with
trespassed tact?

The font I use, a keepsake
pollen clogs my thought.
Metallic taste shifts intervals
between flecks of conversation.
Upload these differences.
Forgive the sobriquets,
slick with indifference,
transposing omniphones and sass
like rogue spurts over the morning PA.

Fluidity, a rancid cusp, is this
brass bell that lets go voice
reptilian as city hall
replete with blueprints
given to the candidates
before election.

She Weaves

She sat, basket between her knees,
a work-in-progress, the tall sweet grass
harvested from the fields
in her memory.
Dark brown children,
toasted by the sun, rip,
run, carefree,
no knowledge yet
of their history.
Hands fly in rudimentary rhythm,
accompanied by the hum
of winged things
who bore witness
just in case
woven baskets ever
found themselves full
of rewritten lies
spread by ocean merchants
whose dark brown bounty
lost almost everything
while laying prone,
stacked and tethered
across the sea
except for the scent
of sweet grass, the rhythm
of hands weaving places
where life could collect
until children could run
and knees could hold
works-in-progress
laced blade by blade
with reality.

Didi Menendez

The Elephant in the Room

It starts with the bagpipes.
The distant sound of horses'
hooves, the wind shuffling
through the birches. Young
men running naked through
the thorny bushes.

A girl drawing John Lennon on
a cardboard. Her mother weaving
threads through a Singer sewing
machine stopping to oil the crank.
The squeaky bottle spilling a drop
onto a garment.

A cough.

The gray sorrowful faces
from the television.
Memorizing the lyrics to a
Beatles' song. *Rocky Raccoon*.
Gideon's Bible.

Her father's razors rusty.
Phlegm coughed up and spit
to the walls. Her father heavy
pacing the halls. Her mother
mopping the floors.

The woodwinds trailing,
the bagpipes whirling,
the boy next door sitting under
a mango tree. An old man
raking the leaves.

A dog whimpering.
A train whistle abandoning.
The sad faces in the television
witnessing. The hum of the
air conditioner. Your sister
shivering. Your father's soiled
underwear in the laundry basket.

Barbara Moore

Shipshape

I don't think I can find you
here in the darkening afternoon
under the faithless cowlick clouds.
I sense you before I see your face,
before I see the back of your head,
before I see your shoulders slump
and roll up again in sets of 10.
You are exercising your right
to exorcise the tension from your frame.

You are getting shipshape
for a boat that has already sailed.
I have stayed behind hopping
because I do not dare to hope
for anything less or more
than what my body
can perform soloing
on one foot first
then on the other.

Terraforming #2

Giddy weeping trees swing sideways, there
goes summer, there goes the night's dark
soldiers dipped in paraffin, painted black,
little red nailpolish eyeholes all along the
perimeter, so silent not even whispering
for 20 years, nothing but backbone and
fingers turning crisp pages unearthed
after last war.

I remember. A roaring campfire and up there,
night sky so brilliant. You can't see this
in the city, no, and you're erasing yourself
anyway, trying to get to some solid core.
Before we sleep, arrangements made,
compartmentalized.
You know this is done. The shuffle of logic, and
know what to bury.

She Drinks

more than she needs
talks about quitting but
can't

bemoans the stupor
established on her
tongue

wants to love but
doesn't find any real
reason

needs a little time
to recoup the heart
undone

says she'll call
soon as the big day
occurs

as if a tiny tiger w/no
teeth at all still can't
shred me

might as well vacuum
the hall fix the playground
have kids

might as well shout at the
wind wonder god's intentions
gesticulate

Floaters

slim chances
in my fat eyes
accumulate like daily dust
in anything ornate

they're in every striation
of my irises
every movement
of the vitreous gel
until all i can see
is the worst that can happen

my mother told me
when i was delivered
the nurse said i was born
with a blue veil over my head
that cellular debris
would give me second sight

later
someone in a sunday suit
looked at me in the back seat
of my father's car
and told me about my eyes

he couldn't see
they were crowded already

muddy buffalo river

muddy buffalo river, rolling like brown snake through green hills, twisting down chert rock escarpment just short of the duck river fall, highway 13 winding out of small town across river to another small town, old storefront glass gleaming in summer sun, wooden boardwalk along one section of town, ancient place where once mules tied to posts in front, trade day yahooing, dogs sold and knives swapped, tales told around bottles of fizzing "shine,"

boy growing up there, trekking hill trails and hollows, fishing cane, dog at heels, mindful of big rattlers sunning by the pathway, cottonmouth moccasins lurking in willows by river bank, hawks spiraling above sun-reflected water looking for prey, falling like a dive bomber, wings folded, grasping unfortunate snake, fish, in powerful talons,

stories of ghosts by the old cemetery on the hillside, white swatches in the night, midnight howling beasts unknown, strange cold touch on the neck in passing, dark night, hair raising, chill bumps standing, blood surging cold song in ears, heart crashing like jackhammer beating concrete, tearing down city of safety, building village of fear,

old days gone, no more, trails covered in foliage, hawks of summer sky long dead and dust, snake's spent skin blending with clay dirt, young boy now old man, stumbling toward graveyard, hoping to be ghost in midnight black, frighten voyagers centuries hence, create sweet bundle of memories to carry to own graves.

47

Belinda Subraman

Freud's Last Poem

A hand waves help
in whispering smoke__

Walls breathe, hum, snore.
Ears echo inward__

Joy outweighs confusion
on this dark park ride,
descending__

Your cold blade in summer sun
expands vulnerability.
Your gravity holds me.
I love your weakness__

Andy Darlington

In Penny Lane there *Is* a Barber shaving customers
(visiting Liverpool, July 2014)

I wasn't here
this never happened
rumours of a distant war
once resented, now embedded
once blood-raw, now no more,
an endless autopsy, a history tour
a heritage trail, a legacy project,
when it all comes down to this
laminated into a tourist map
a twist in a leisure industry
frozen reconstructions of
memory-distort on pause
in a national misTrust,
no stylus bites play-in,
days blur on the flip-side,
it was light, it was dark
this sad escapology
eradicates every scratch,
yet I'm here on Mathew St
where once it happened,
just six decades too late
squint ears to catch echoes
of screams on the screen
see these walking dead,
this never happened
I wasn't here,
I'm still trapped
somewhere in this photo…

Give Up the Sun

Dear_____,

I know it's been a while since you've heard from me
and I hope you've been able to forgive all past trans-
gressions. Friends are friends, right? Alright,
maybe I don't have a pot to piss in. I'm just hoping
against hope that you're a better person than me.

To explain to you where I am let's just stay it's stucco,
okay? It's in America. Does that help? I'm scraping
the couch cushions for that lousy 40 that'll be
the bright spot of my week.

The heat is dismal and walking through the air, day
or night, is like slogging through butter. Two lanes
of blacktop stretch out into oblivion. Oblivion and a
dense treeline. Suzi and Dolores will be out working
the blacktop later. The Abortion says it misses you.
Sonic booms overhead. Servicemen every weekend.
Endless drone of cicadas

Love and kisses

In Buffalo

home is where they know your father
wasn't he a character

not really from here
not really from Buffalo

Buffalo, there's a tough corner
Buffalo, they don't mess around in Buffalo

city of wet bricks, patched-up asphalt
home, where you're part of the environment

it's still the Anchor Bar for wings
for beef-on-weck, that's tricky

home-cooking, fried bologna, red sauce
flavored with mint, tuna and peas on toast

take the train to Collegetown
watch John Cassavetes movies, hear poetry

every line with a kick
like a Rockette, ready for her big break

every line doesn't have to be funny
I would kill to be in Buffalo

inside an appalachian ditch with the farther along blues

strictly apocryphal shenanigans except for the occasional
forever which was me in places no one could reach down

far enough to groove a sputtering sarcasm. mirrors on the
other side of the bar point out all the reasons i'm planted

in vinyl instead of sifting ohio farmland for salt of the earth.
my hand is wrapped around a distance i created but don't

know how to find my way back to. religious icon candles have
burned my fingerprints off. unnumbered reckoning has

me hunkering down below any mental infractions in
the witch grass searching out a sealed with never be missed

but we take our wows whenever we can get them. my right
eye is blue & my left eye is red. either i went down fighting

or i'm seeing the world as it is as well as it isn't. a realist
manifesto greased with butterfly paste is passed my way

via egocentric scuttlebutt which isn't set on self-destruct
but self-construction without an inflatable id. six days on

the road & foolish enough to believe i'll get seven days
to undo the damage. you can call me a dreamer or call me

a romantic. you can call me a naive optimist albeit with
a candy-coated chip on my shoulder. once semantic

differences have become inexplicably connected. if
inexplicable is possible in this age of information. crawlers

are detaining the latter while pawing the former then switch
places because intent should be the first question not the last.

Cee Williams

The Seedier Side of Pollination

I would write
love poems
to you about
the sex life of plants

flowers and
pollen transference
stamen and pistils
and such. Articulations

on lateral
and median
nectaries. Stigmas,
styles, ovules

ovaries,
sepals,
petals inveigling honeybees

honeybees, worker bees,
queen, drones,
pheromones

odd little
poems
plush green,

black soil,
jade hummingbirds,
fat earthworms, roots
stems, leaves

sun blushed hush
quiet enough
to hear celestial breaths
swell fruit, stretch vines

sky worshiping branches
entranced,
enchanted

odd
little
love poems to you

doomed to be
pecked at by grackles
and sparrows
devoured,

shat out into forgotten meadows

embedded in decaying leaves
and dying grass
and earthen sheets
and winter's sleep

and winter's sleep
deep acacia root
useless milkweed
bitter acorn flour

seedy
little
love

poems
full of
sexy

words like germination
anther, filament
protandry

it would be
in my
nature

to write to you
of such things
to liken you

to spring
all bards sing
to call the birds

every lover praises nectar
every poem
a sacramental
testament ancient as

honeycombs

I would write
love poems
to you about
honeycombs

full of
sexy words
like

royal jelly.

A perpetual clash between imagination & system that spawned
tricked out reality has fixed hierarchy. encourages us to live
dangerously – though constantly reminding us of bent framework
& the steel plate in our head that could collapse on impact.
envelopes poetic disordering of the senses while making holy
nods illegal even to savior's son. in a stroke of disingenuous
calamity an enchanting mess becomes transparent irony.
preaching revolution of love though we live every single day
of our life under the supposed threat of unpardonable sin.
demanding us to become obsessed with death. knuckling
under to obvious implications. a picture of heavily made up
trustworthy in order to give us hope. but it's giving me the willies.
sudden italics sweep us off our feet. take us either to a bed of
poppies or drop our digs on where it will all end. a painted backdrop
is only an imitation of life that's pleasant viewing nevertheless – like
quickly extinguished sulfur scent or a wretched beginning conjuring
up tomorrow. warning obsession with the truth is bad medicine.
encouraged to feel free to unfold the soul under the pretense
of both spiritual awakening & carnal pleasure. offering something
for nothing which is romantic myth at its most fatal flutter.
bucket on the bitch.. must kill this confusion. will drink water
and tea till ringing stops. senses are open. too open. i smell
things that aren't even in the house. i'm hungry for flesh. not
death/but sex. she's unreachable. that's worse to me than being
alone. need an ok. a permanent tattoo of approval. see horrific
dance behind eyes. afraid to sleep. afraid to write. afraid to play
channels with music or the tv holding all these netflix movie film
blackmail. maybe 2014 will bring nut house. the stay i've always
wanted. will keep tinfoil hat on or draw blood. yellow room. green
bed. squeak of rusty springs. injections of dream. stuffing anger into
the black like a muskets kill. vincent price on my head. painted up
like a true madhouse. maybe I'm all oranges and no apples. the doctor
will be angry. no matter. there's worse waiting for me if this train
stays on these tracks! Aaaaaahhhhhhhh..

58

delectable fabric is found in the gutters. under stars
a wheelchair roams legless though still flashes
the beige whites remaining. an old structure gets a
facelift. progress isn't. an optical illusion is ebbing
tide of tent city. rolling on a current to stockyard
oases of depraved. out of sight doesn't mean not
there. igniting mind explosion with no conscience while
operating the bone machine with eyes closed. staggering
the totality with a left hook which hasn't learned to fall
in the right direction. gliding over maddening course of
events mapped out ahead of time as well as space.
shadows come to life. contemplate taking yours. wind blows
cooled urine past urban nostril twenty stories from
redevelopment. watching sixteen in skintight skin will get
you twenty isn't a crime but could be a first step in that
direction. seven'll get you rave happy though a funny tip
of a cap & look towards an innocuous van is a sure sign
christmas doesn't fall in january. not about to turn around now.
not when beating the demons at their own game. banking on
another plan in flight is like breaking the trumpeted glass swan.
not afraid to twist the head off if need be. not afraid of ruffling
some feathers. putting kibosh on assassination before the naive
innocently wander into the mouth of the pseudo-revelatory
beast. into the grip of derailed demonology while loved ones

are frantically searching for any soundtrack but grand finale
in e minor. not that rave is an activity to which i aspire.
rendering enhancement a nonstarter. though odd thought
can be a mundane observation in wee hours. the square has
been sanitized for company. the door is locked. sealed shut
as a youth born to fear & loathing though still capable of
peeling a banana from a rotten apple. simple is finding
life in the dying. difficult is having eyes for such minor detail.
a shadow follows my train of thought. or does the train follow
the shadow. it's certainly not behind a white dress. a minor due
paid to truth in advertising. however it's been said that alabaster
just might be the hot color in another season or two in what
would prove an unacceptable dichotomy. gutter & legless
wheelchair have no chance. the fabric is no longer tender
& menacing at once. sweet juice of life is set to be sugar free.
tofu yoga mat & velvet rope sickening. even forgotten alleys
balk at the notion. angels flight was a sagacious title. they're
fleeing. new cat in the house ratlike. though the former has
an uncanny resemblance to the latter. now jamming the
airwaves with human kindness. pirate radio blasting from
mount sinai. knocking cruel intentions from under their crowns.
beating the rigged system like a rented mule. my synapses snapping
like uncovered live wires.

More Than Food, More Than Clothes

When I come back
I will be
Lily of the Field
I will not want
when I come back
honey bees will
tickle my sex
when I come
home ape will
morph into apis
reconstitute
abandoned boxes
nano crystalline palaces
holoquantum phalluses
will catch us the foxes
the little foxes
for our vineyards
will be in bloom
too dumb to tell
lilium from opium
stepped on or not
so just please
when I come home
wake me not.

Jeff Filipski

Every Poem Is A Paradox
by Ron Androla

It's bright Sunday morning jazz radio
On the dresser by the open window
Overlooking the flat, new garage roof;
Over the corners, wild trees & their
Perfect city birds. I've adjusted why
Don't we fall in love down to stereo
The warbles & the shrieks so I hear
Music & life together. The warbles
& the shrieks & the church bells &
Trains, rusty zippers of weak jets.
In a small eggshell sky window
The traffic is an ironic pterodactyl.
We're smack dab in the middle,
& we swing alone as we tumble
Out of dead people & back into
Dead people.
As we roll we marry & work &
Party & collapse & sing.

October 2014

PRESSURE PRESS COLLECTION 2014

Lightning Source UK Ltd.
Milton Keynes UK
UKRC021342111019
351394UK00005B/98

9781320179782